YO-EGI-232

NFTs

Table of Contents

NFTs

Introduction

The modern gold rush is happening right now. NFTs, or non-fungible tokens, have taken the internet by storm. Artists who hadn't been able to make much money before are now pocketing millions of dollars on their crafts.

In turn, collectors are walking away from online marketplaces with digital art worth millions more as the artist grows in importance and worldwide availability.

But the NFT craze isn't limited to just digital art. Sports cards are now sports *moments* with movement and sound, and each one is unique and one of a kind. That simple fact is causing collectors to reach deep into their pockets to pull out millions of dollars without a second thought.

No one knows how long the whole thing will last, but one thing we do know: If you can jump into the NFT scene quickly, you stand a fair chance at walking away with a good chunk of change.

However, there are some pitfalls to beware of. Any time a million dollars is at stake, there are precautions to take and shady people to watch out for. But there's so much more to gain if one takes the right precautions and does the research into viable options.

The purpose of this book is to help you get into the NFT arena as quickly as possible and get cash flowing.

Do we promise you that you will make a million dollars using this book? No.

Can you make a million dollars going on the information in this book? Yes.

People with no guidance at all are cashing in on the NFT phenomenon. So, if the people who don't have a book to show them the way are raking in cash, you stand a solid chance yourself if you're even more educated regarding NFTs, their availability, and where and how to cash in on this growing phenomenon.

What you'll gain from this book

You might be surprised at how tech-savvy you do not have to be to get involved in the NFT scene.

This book considers the possibility that the reader doesn't know anything about NFTs other than the fact that they inhabit a million-dollar market right now. This book will not claim to be the only authority on the subject you will ever need, but we do promise that we will tell you everything you need to know for the moment to dip your toes into the pool to get started. There are lots of things about NFTs—blockchains, tokens, and the like—that have nothing to do with making you a million dollars but that any investor needs to be aware of before starting out. Our goal is to get you equipped and active so you can start getting your hand in the arena for a chance to grab at your own pile of cash.

I will especially help you know what to look for so that you're not separated from your money by somebody who knows how to play the system at someone else's expense. I'll also show you how to reduce the risk of your money and your NFT evaporating into thin air. (Yes, this happens.)

Okay, so let's start knowing so you can get going.

Chapter 1: What are NFTs, and how can you take advantage of them?

What are NFTs?

If you're of a certain age, you remember when one-of-a-kind items sold for big figures. Limited-edition tennis shoes fetched ridiculous numbers. Ridiculous as in good. Barbie dolls that saw a limited run, or even consisted of just one doll, were hotly sought after, and to this day, people are pulling out their toys, their shoes, their models that are unopened and still in their original packages, and collectors are paying the prices that the sellers are demanding.

Why? Because there was only one. There was only one in that condition or make, or they are so limited that collectors horde them. The rarer or scarcer the item, the more collectible it was, and the more money people were willing to fork over. Nothing about that has changed; tangible objects are still just as valuable as once before. However, the whole NFT phenomenon is the next step in that logic. They are the newest wave of collectibles in the modern age.

NFTs are essentially *digital* collectibles. They are one of a kind, and they represent a wide spectrum of digital assets.

So, what exactly has the potential to be an NFT? The answer is pretty simple. If it can be stored digitally, it can be an NFT.

No, really.

JPEGS, GIFs, tweets, videos, songs, video game collectible items.

The potential for items that can be sold as NFTs is mind-blowing because it's limitless. I can see the gears turning in your head.

But hold on... Why buy a digital painting for obscene amounts of money when you can do a quick search for the same image and download it? Well, you can visit the museum and look at the *Mona Lisa*. You can take a picture of it yourself or find an HD image of it online. But neither of those scenarios ends with you owning the *Mona Lisa*—just a copy.

Digital assets that ascend to NFT status are *not* copies; they are originals. They are endowed with originality thanks to the technology that brought us fungible tokens like bitcoin and dogecoin. They're given an electronic fingerprint by being attached to a digital token that qualifies them as the original item. When it's bought, ownership changes hands, and the buyer has certain rights, depending on what they've purchased.

For example, take the first-ever tweet on Twitter. It sold for a gasping 2.9 million dollars. You could easily hop on your browser and view the same tweet without a penny leaving your bank account. But the person who forked over all that money now owns that tweet in a format that has a unique data signature. No matter how you screenshot, copy and paste, or right-click and save, you will never "own" that maiden voyage tweet the same way the buyer owns it.

So, if you could get to a place where you could sell your tweets, you'd surely keep the bills paid. So how do you cash in on this?

How can you take advantage of NFTs?

Did your mind go straight to money? That's an obvious benefit to leverage, but the advantages of NFTs go beyond dollars and cents. However, we'll start with money first.

The market for NFTs definitely has the potential to shorten your creation-to-salesfloor cycle by eliminating the need for a physical product. Many NFTs are works of digital art. If you carved out your own corner of the digital art market, you could skip the steps of ordering prints or setting up an online print shop. Sure, you would have to step up production of original works but not having to buy and handle anything physical changes the sales market completely? Think about it.

Game developers are hot for the raw potential of the NFT market. Consider—*World of Warcraft* is already pulling in money from subscription packages. Imagine if in-game items were unique, un-copied, and could be bought and sold *outside* of the game as if they were real, tangible assets. You could possess the only diamond sword with a polished dragon bone hilt across the entire virtual universe.

Forget game items… How about games themselves? Think about a Nintendo game that existed only as an NFT, and to play it, you had to buy it? And no one else owned it—you had the exclusive rights to that digital media.

But it's not all about the visual media, either. High-profile musicians have already released NFT-only music albums. In a world where everyone buys digital copies of the original music, the buyer of an NFT album has exclusive bragging rights that come with ownership. It's the equivalent of an album that has the artist's signature and a personal message saying, "This is yours and nobody else's! Thanks!"

Making commissions from NFTS

Depending on the kind of NFTs you produce, you stand a chance at making lifetime commissions from them, provided your work becomes collectible and tradeable.

In the digital age, you won't have to worry about waiting for a phone call from the people doing business in order to get what is due to you. A nifty thing called smart contracts ensures the seller gets paid automatically when their NFTs switch hands to the new owner.

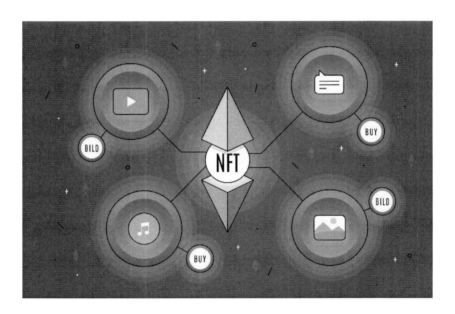

Chapter 2: NFTs and the blockchain

It is easy to neglect learning about blockchain technology since that isn't where your spending power resides. But cryptocurrency would have no value and zero spending power without the blockchain. In turn, this logically means that NFTs have no value without the blockchain as well.

So what is a blockchain, and how does it work?

With a traditional bank, you have an accountant who oversees the final records of all transactions and balances all the numbers in the accounts. They're assisted by accounting software, for sure, but there is always a middleman between the financial institution and the outside world, and all the money that comes and goes does so through that accountant's authority. The numbers are the accountant's to approve or deny.

A blockchain contains records of every single transaction that takes place on it. The blockchain is often compared to a ledger, which is accurate; only a blockchain is digital with no physical accountant. These transactions on the blockchain are all public and viewable, so no accountant is overseeing and adjusting numbers. The ledger takes care of itself, and if anyone has any questions, they can view the financial records.

That's the short picture. However, we're going to make sure you can completely grasp the concept of a blockchain and what it does so you can become an expert in NFTs.

How does a blockchain work?

As mentioned before, a blockchain is a publicly viewable list of transactions for a particular item or NFT. So the Bitcoin blockchain has an indelible record of every time bitcoin was sent or received. This is the core mechanic of every cryptocurrency.

In order to keep the transaction records on a blockchain accurate so that there's no need for a human to play watchdog, the accuracy of a blockchain is perpetually being verified, which is the power-consuming aspect of cryptocurrency. It also requires a vast amount of computing power. This is accomplished by a gigantic peer-to-peer network of computers. The computers check and secure the blockchain's accuracy 24/7, and the software used to do it is open-source.

Why would you use your computer for such a power-intensive process when so many people are already doing this? The answer is simple and can be rewarding. The more you contribute your own computing power to the upkeep of the blockchain, the more you're rewarded a measure of digital currency for your troubles. This is where Bitcoin mining comes from.

Thanks to this "auto-ledger" aspect of the blockchain, it enables people to make business transactions anywhere for anything without the say of a financial institution or without providing sensitive information like names and card information. Anonymity is a huge part of the appeal of cryptocurrency. A blockchain transaction is more secure than a traditional debit or credit transaction. There is zero risk of your financial information being compromised or stolen.

At first, the thought of there being nobody in control of balancing numbers might be unsettling. It might look like a ship with nobody at the helm. But the other side of the coin (See what we did there?) is that it also means there is no one who can change, falsify, or manipulate records. The digital accounting ledger is unchangeable.

All the peer-to-peer computers supporting a blockchain cannot alter any of the data on the blockchain. The information can only be verified, not altered. Nobody can lie to you about transactions and numbers—the date is all readily available.

What that means for NFTs

How often have people bought a priceless work of art only to discover later that it was a forgery? The fact that an NFT utilizes the blockchain to both exist and move means that it is impossible to create a counterfeit NFT. The record of the NFT is indelibly on display for all the world to see on the blockchain it lives on.

If someone is selling you an NFT for $7 million, you can look it up on the blockchain to verify its legitimacy.

Some blockchains are more than just ledgers. Ethereum, for example, is also a powerful software platform that allows users to play games on it. One of them involves buying and selling virtual property with real cryptocurrency. Ethereum is a technology that is home to not only games, but also to digital currency, global payments, and numerous types of applications. It's a community with its own digital economy where creators can earn online, but it doesn't stop there. The limits to Ethereum only stop when its inhabitants quit creating. It's available to anyone in the world with internet access.

Chapter 3: A brief history of NFTs

The exact history of NFTs—where they came from and why—has some flexibility. Here we'll cover multiple angles and tellings of the genesis of NFTs.

What circumstances led to the creation of NFTs?

Combing through Google to find resources to answer this question reveals several interesting narratives. The first one is the most fascinating: That NFTs arose from the needs of artists in an increasingly digital art scene to be able to protect themselves and their work from theft and plagiarism.

The year was 2014. Tumblr culture was at an all-time peak. It was an excellent way to have your digital works of art seen since everyone was sharing digital art far and wide on the platform in an effort to get noticed and possibly sell originals. The problem was that the scene was big on inspiration and short on recognition. Sharing your work on Tumblr was like throwing a physical painting into a whirlwind and hoping someone caught it and linked it back to the artist. The poster had no idea where the work was going to go or if anyone who saw it would recognize it as yours. It was easy to steel the concept and modify or recreate it as your own.

Similarly, the works of artists were being shared far and wide, but their credentials weren't. The artists' names didn't have a fraction of the reach that their pieces did, and they certainly had no control over who shared their work with who, which also limited the monetary compensation an artist might have received had their work received the credit it was due.

If artists were going to exercise their legal rights over their artwork or have any say in how their works were used, something would have to change in the digital world.

Who invented NFTs?

According to an article in *The Atlantic*, two individuals in the digital art scene got their heads together to find a way to regain control over art and give it back to the creators. Anil Dash, who is now the CEO of Glitch, paired up with artist, Kevin McCoy, for an event that was supposed to generate new ideas by connecting artists and technologists. The talents of both people bled together and became the spawning pool that would eventually birth the idea that would lead to the NFTs blowing up the market today.

What? You mean to say that they had something in mind other than money?

McCoy had been giving some thought to the way blockchains were an indelible ledger of all digital transactions that transpired on them. Whatever happened on them left an unchangeable trail—breadcrumbs back to the originator. Theoretically, if an artist's work were connected to a blockchain and given a unique means of identification, then the artist could see everywhere it went and the end user could trace it back to where it originated from.

One super-late day in the wee hours of the morning, the two men had a wobbly prototype of their idea. They gave it a working name of "monetized graphics," even though money wasn't their aim at the time. They were only interested in giving artists control—a digital footprint to track their work.

The proof of concept came with McCoy putting a video clip on a blockchain called *Namecoin*, and Dash bought it for $4.00.

Their idea must have been *too* innovative because it didn't catch on right away. Dash had written off the project as a footnote in internet history. If only they had known, right?

The alternate narrative of colored coins

Where the story of Dash and McCoy starts in 2014, the more embryonic origin story starts in 2012 without art being involved.

Colored coins were born out of the realm of the cryptocurrency Ethereum. (Remember that little online ecosphere we talked about earlier that has limitless potential for creativity and growth?) If crypto totally blew up, there would need to be a way to use the blockchain for collectibles, property, company shares, coupons, and other things in and out of the digital realm. This necessity called for a medium of exchange that wasn't neutral and that wasn't fungible.

So colored coins came on the scene as Bitcoin tokens with more to them than the underlying properties of plain Bitcoin. The fun part was that colored coins made use of the already existing Bitcoin infrastructure, so the innovation didn't call for anything extra, it simply expanded what was available at the time.

Colored coins ultimately didn't last, but some credit them as the "origin movie" that would lay the groundwork for the innovations of Dash and McCoy that followed a couple of years later.

What are some noteworthy NFTs?

Whichever narrative you put your faith in, it's clear that the internet discovered ways of capitalizing on a digital asset that couldn't be replicated. Following are some of the landmark NFTs that demonstrated what was possible.

#1. The first tweet on Twitter

We've already touched on this, but we need to look at some of the details. The tweet was sold to Sina Estav, the CEO of Bridge Oracle. But the tweet will continue to exist on Twitter, and the blockchain technology allows Estav to have received the NFT as "signed and verified" by Jack Dorsey.

#2. Doge

Memes are everywhere. They are less than a dime a dozen. A few have had enough staying power to remain in the popular consciousness despite the ADHD of the internet. One of them is certainly the Shiba Inu that became the face of Dogecoin.

While Dogecoin itself is still valued at less than $1.00, the original meme sold for a staggering 1,696.9 ETH (Ethereum trading currency).

#3 Metarift

Metarift was a mesmerizing three-dimensional sculpture created by the artist who creates under the pseudonym Pak. Metarift is a looping video of a group of highly reflective spheres cocooned within the infinity symbol. It's not much different than any other abstract animated GIF that you would find on the internet, except this one is endowed with the uniqueness and the non-fungibility you would expect of an NFT. The value of this NFT was perceived as being so high that it sold for $904,413.

#4 *Everydays—The first 5000 days*

As of this writing, Beeple is one of the digital artists breaking the NFT scene with record-worthy sales. Beeple made an image that was a collage of art that Beeple had made every day since May 2007 called, *Everydays—The first 5000 days*. Not a single day was excluded from the image. That single collective piece of digital artwork sold for over $69 million.

#5 Forever Rose

What kind of roses do you give on Valentine's Day? Somebody got the gift of a piece of digital artwork depicting a gorgeous red rose against a black background. The image had been made into an NFT, and it sold for $1 million. It is a safe bet that somebody out there isn't complaining about how much their significant other spends on them.

#6 The Potato

The artist, Kevin Abosch, who created and sold the Forever Rose NFT? He also sold a photograph of a potato to a businessman for 1 million euros.

Who has used NFTs the most?

As a whole, artists and celebrities have been the fastest to jump on the NFT explosion.

Rapper Snoop Dogg released an NFT that takes the buyer on a journey through Snoop's memories from his early years, some artwork, and an original track that is appropriately titled "NFT."

Skater Tony Hawk transformed a video of him performing his last ever 540-degree ollie into an NFT. What makes it so special is that fans will see the last footage of him performing the trick. So the blockchain token isn't the only thing that makes it special.

Even celebrities who have kept a low profile have been cashing in. Lindsay Lohan minted her own token on wearable, netting a tidy $50,000. She released another single on Fans Forever. The song itself can be streamed pretty much anywhere you get your music, but the NFT version has exclusive visuals.

Sports celebrities such as the NFL four-time Super Bowl Champion, Rob Gronkowski, have minted their own NFTs in the form of digital trading cards. His try at the whole NFT thing gained him 1.6 million in Ethereum cryptocurrency.

Between artwork and music and strange combinations of the two, plus videos, trading cards, and so much more, NFTs are not limited in what they can be. The only limit in the creation of new NFTs is the minds that create them. It's also clear that they're not limited in how much they can earn.

The next section in this book looks at ongoingly popular and collectible NFTs.

Chapter 4: What are some of the most popular NFTs?

Following are three popular NFTs ranging from virtual pets to video games to art to real estate. The concepts are limitless if you can find an audience willing to virtually breed, trade, or buy and sell your collectible good. If you have a niche interest, there is likely an equally interested crowd out there to purchase or participate in it. All you have to do is digitize it and find the market.

CryptoKitties

You'd think the Pokémon franchise would have gotten in on this first, but nope. Virtual cats beat everyone to the punch. Each CryptoKitty is unique, different, and rather than idly taking up bandwidth, they can be bred together, with each kitty containing digital DNA. The series is worth millions of dollars, and it was so popular in 2017 that the Ethereum blockchain was brought to a grinding halt due to the traffic that CryptoKitties generated.

CryptoPunks

Retro video games seem to be enjoying a comeback, and the aesthetic is especially cherished. Pixel art is in the art community at large. But can you imagine laying down over $7 million for a piece of this low-res, blocky art? Installments in the CryptoPunks series command ridiculous numbers when they sell. And they aren't even games. They're collectible works of art done in the blocky, pixelated style of past video games. No two are alike, and they're given all the special identifiers of an NFT. CryptoPunk #7804 sold for 4,200 ETH or $7,570,000.

Virtual Real Estate

Ethereum is more than digital currency. The network houses a virtual world game where players buy and sell property. An estate in the game sold for $1.5 million. Imagine leaving that as an inheritance for a loved one.

There are more instances of NFTs making huge profits, but we've covered enough to make the point. A quick Google search will render you thousands of examples if you'd like to continue exploring the types of things that have made money in this ever-growing digital marketplace. In the minds of people with the money to spend, NFTs are real, and they make real money. It is a multi-billion dollar industry that has sprung up seemingly overnight like mushrooms after a heavy rain, and everyone is trying to get in on the latest craze.

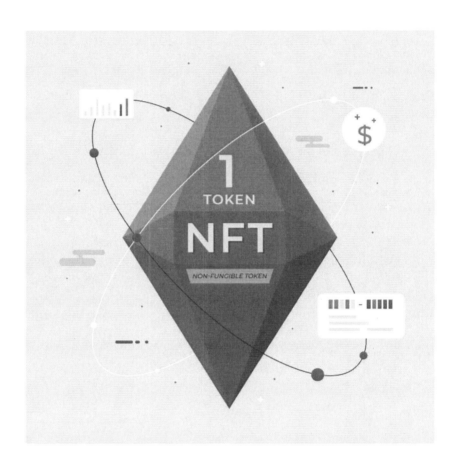

Chapter 5: How do NFTs work?

Every non-fungible token consists of two parts. There is the token that lives on the blockchain, and then there is the asset itself, whether it's a piece of digital art, a video, or any other kind of digital asset.

Blockchains are grossly energy inefficient while they're taking care of tokens and cryptocurrency alone, so the energy demands are part of the reason that digital assets are not stored on the blockchain along with the token that points to them.

Any other token on the blockchain, such as Bitcoin, would be defined by its value rather than its unique characteristics. It's the opposite with NFTs. They are defined by their unique properties rather than any innate value. The value of NFTs is that they are at the mercy of what people are willing to pay for them as are most collectibles.

So, it's the token, not the digital asset, that determines the uniqueness of the NFT. This is where some people get hung up on just how valuable NFTs truly are.

It's also the NFT, not the digital asset, that is securely stored and indelibly recorded on the blockchain. This is where some people get hung up on just how secure ownership of an NFT truly is. Because it is possible for the asset to cease to exist while the token exists for as long as the blockchain does.

For example, if you bought a tweet that was minted as an NFT, that tweet would not be stored on the blockchain with the token. It would also remain on Twitter. However, if, for some reason, Twitter shut down, your digital asset would go with it. The NFT you purchased would not bring it back, and there is no tangible asset to hold claim to.

Something else that happens is that unscrupulous individuals will mint copyrighted digital assets as NFTs and sell them. If you're unfortunate enough to buy such a thing, and the government comes along and seizes the digital asset under the pretense of copyright law, your ownership of the token on the blockchain will not protect you.

Still, this has not discouraged people from finding ways of monetizing NFTs, investing in NFTs, and collecting them as one-of-a-kind and unique items.

The question of what you truly own

This is the part where logic and abstract thinking and philosophy all collide because it all depends on the virtual value and availability of the NFT.

The value of cryptocurrency alone was hotly debated when it was a new thing. Many skeptics regarded it as imaginary money. After all, if you couldn't hold it or put it in a vending machine, what case could you make that it was even real?

It is a psychological rabbit hole you can go down into and never reach the bottom. Many concepts that people regard as concrete realities are just as intangible. Friendship, love, fear, or how about a marriage license? Does a marriage license guarantee your ownership of somebody else's heart? The only thing the license guarantees is that you have some legal recourse when things don't go as planned. The intangible realities represented by that license, things that cannot be governed or controlled by that license, are things that could be construed as not being real in the first place. But they're very real to many people, and they build their lives around them.

So just as a marriage license, a driver's license, a hunting license, a business contract, or a deed to a tract of land all point to intangible things that can't be quantified, so a non-fungible token on a blockchain points to something of value that a buyer or a collector could cherish very much. If it's real to them, then it's real enough.

And as someone looking to get in on the NFT craze, if they're willing to spend money on NFTs that you create, then it's real enough.

Chapter 6: What can NFTs be used for?

Uses for NFTs is as endless as the mind that create them.

Images

These can be photographs, digital paintings, or any other sort of media stored in JPEG format. GIFs would fall under this category as well.

Videos

Clips, music videos, and even full-length movies are joining the NFT army. Certain features are unlocked and available only to the purchaser.

Music Albums

Remember the days when some releases were CD-only? The next evolution of that seems to be releases that are NFT-only. Artists release special editions with extras not available anywhere else in NFT formats.

Apps

Imagine if Microsoft Paint were released as an NFT and put across as being *the original* Microsoft Paint. How many millions do you think that could rake in? That's the direction that NFT apps are heading.

Games

Forget Microsoft Paint... what if *Minesweeper* from the early days of Windows was tokenized and marketed as the original *Minesweeper*? But NFT games go beyond vintage. Some developers that have the gravity are releasing NFT-only games, and people are buying them. And that doesn't even include the market for in-game items that can be tokenized and traded outside the boundaries of the games themselves.

Proof of Ownership

The NFT scene is gradually coming around to noticing the application of NFTs to legal matters or other situations where accuracy and indent ability of information is crucial. Imagine marriage licenses, deeds to lands and properties, and other such things being tokenized and forever residing on the blockchain until the end of time. Or at least until the end of the blockchain. It would be a record that could not be tampered with by anyone.

This opens the door to a discussion of smart contracts. Since the information can't be changed by anyone, it's quite possible that smart contracts could be used in place of lawyers. They could eventually automate the release of payments from escrow accounts once both parties honor their agreements.

For everything that NFTs have been used for, the latent potential they still hold is monumental.

Chapter 7: What is fungibility?

It almost sounds like a cross between "fun" and "vegetable." But no, it doesn't mean that nonfungible items can't have fun with vegetables. It's a meaning that is centered around an item's uniqueness or lack thereof.

Defining Fungibility

Fungible: (Of goods contracted for without an individual specimen being specified) able to replace or be replaced by another identical item; mutually interchangeable.

Or more plainly...

Suppose you have a 1975 quarter in your pocket. Also, suppose that I like to collect 1975 quarters. I propose that I trade your 1975 quarter for my 1983 quarter. We both walk away from the transaction, neither richer nor poorer, because coins are fungible commodities. They can be traded. They have equal value. The extra value that I assigned to the date printed on the quarter has no bearing on the quarter's real-world value. They are of equal value, so they exchange just fine; therefore, they are fungible.

Now, suppose that you and I both collect baseball cards or Pokémon cards. Different cards demand different prices on the market depending on the card's scarcity, condition, and other factors. If I want to trade one card of mine for a different card of yours, you'd think twice since they obviously aren't of equal value. These cards are non-fungible. Trading them would mean a change in the value of our assets when we walk away.

Fungibility in crypto

Are you with us so far? So, suppose I wanted to trade my Bitcoin for yours. Yes, that would be utterly pointless. But for the sake of argument, we could do it and be neither richer nor poorer because Bitcoin is just as fungible as the quarters in our pockets. One Bitcoin equals one Bitcoin, always. Same for Ethereum, Dogecoin, and any other cryptocurrency.

Why are NFTs non-fungible?

Non-Fungible Tokens and Fungible tokens share many characteristics, except for one:

Each NFT is one of a kind. One of my NFTs cannot be exchanged for one of yours without changing the value of our assets, just like the exchange of baseball cards or Pokémon cards. While this sounds like a way of complicating things, it's actually a bonus to you when you do business.

If you have an NFT, it means that there isn't anything like it in the entirety of cyberspace, in the cloud, or in local storage. No other NFT will be able to mimic or replace yours—digitally speaking, of course. This is all thanks to a digital signature assigned to each token on the blockchain.

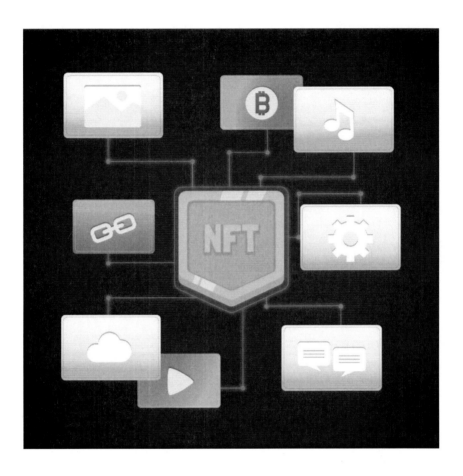

Chapter 8: Where to buy and invest NFTs

It should be noted that there's a difference between an NFT marketplace and the role that the blockchain plays for NFTs. The blockchain supports the financial system that allows you to buy and sell and trade NFTs in the first place. Marketplaces, however, are where everyone comes together to browse, buy, and trade their wares. Marketplaces are like the grocery store while the blockchain is the cashier.

The list of NFT marketplaces is growing, and it's only going to continue to do so. Here's a list of some of the hottest NFT marketplaces and what makes them so special.

Nifty Gateway

Nifty Gateway was put on the map when it hosted the auction where people set a record in NFT sales by selling his painting *CROSSROAD* for a record $6.6 million. Ever since then, Nifty Gateway has been the place to find works by celebrities. When someone famous announces on Twitter that they're about to drop an NFT, Nifty Gateway is usually the place that tweet lands. With that kind of track record, Nifty Gateway has a strong lead in sales records and sales volume.

SuperRare

In sharp contrast to our first listing, there is SuperRare. Art is SuperRare's first priority. And they don't just let anyone in. Less than 1% of all applicants get their foot in the door with this marketplace. They are very highly selective of who they allow in and what they allow displayed. If you're the kind of collector looking for exclusivity and scarcity, this is the marketplace in which to find it.

Just as strongly as SuperRare focuses on art, they also look to build and sustain communities and artists. If you as a creator are privileged enough to get into SuperRare, the work you showcase will not be allowed to be part of any editions. What your feature will be one of one—they only deal in originals. The name of this marketplace is quite literal on what they have to offer.

Async Art

With the rush to create marketplaces in the NFT sphere, Async Art might have actually accomplished something that nobody else has. Async has been developed quite recently in 2020. Their whole premise is programmable art. The NFTs consist of master images that are made up of multiple layers. Buyers can own the master image, but the various layers can also belong to other people. The layers can be altered in different ways so that the master image changes. These can be subject to the whims of the various owners, or they can be affected by things such as weather or cultural conditions.

MakersPlace

If you like the idea of collaborations within the NFT space, then MakersPlace will probably want to talk to you. Especially if you're a celebrity artist. The more high-profile the collaboration project, the better. As a buyer, you are treated to a daily email that makes suggestions for your shopping based on your preferences.

OpenSea, "World's First and Largest NFT Marketplace"

As soon as you visit OpenSea's homepage, you're greeted with a statement that it's the largest and the first NFT Marketplace in the world.

One thing is definitely for certain: They have a wide range of digital goods to select from. There are obviously art and art-related NFTs, but the selection goes so much further. If you want a domain name that cannot easily be censored or censored at all, you can purchase it on OpenSea. If you have a thing for digital trading cards, and not just the sports variety, OpenSea has you covered. Sports-related NFTs and both digital and real-world collectibles are also marketed here.

Gamers will be stopped in their tracks at the sight of over 700 different projects, including games centered around trading cards, around collectibles, some of the collectibles are games themselves, and community-based digital art projects.

Rarible

Rarible prides itself on being community-owned. It has a strong focus on art, but not just showcasing it. This is one of the places you will want to write down as a go-to for minting new NFTs. And it doesn't have to be just artwork. It's also the place to mint NFT books, music albums, and movies. The movies have a special marketing showcase here. They can be set up so that the public has a limited viewing for free, but the full project is viewable only to the buyer.

Foundation

You can only have so many NFT marketplaces that focus on art before they all start to look alike. Foundation has come along with a greater degree of innovation than some of its peers. Yes, it's extremely art-centric, but it's also on a mission as much as it is a marketplace. They don't just want the people using Foundation to try to sell their art. As the site itself says, they want them to hack, subvert, and manipulate the value of created work. They want their users to tinker with the concept of value itself. People who share Foundation's vision for the future are rewarded. When an NFT trades on Foundation, the artist makes a 10% profit on that secondary transaction.

MythMarket

Sometimes you can guess what a marketplace is all about just by its name. MythMarket is a dead giveaway that it's gaming-focused, especially when it comes to trading cards. But you will find some things here that have less in common with gaming. Digital Garbage Pail Kids cards are aplenty here. As are GoPePe trading cards. If you like gaming and you like cards, MythMarket will be one of the first places you stop.

BakerySwap

It would be perfectly possible to sell baked goods as NFTs. But physical baking isn't the aim of BakerySwap.

BakerySwap is many things, but above all, it strives to be a decentralized exchange. More than just a marketplace, it's a crypto hub with a vast array of services. One of these is the fact that it is an NFT supermarket. Many of the services available can be paid for using BAKE tokens. If you're planning on minting your own NFTs, this is another place to write down. On BakerySwap, minting NFTs is simple and straightforward.

KnownOrigin

KnownOrigin isn't just another art-focused marketplace building on exclusivity. KnownOrigin drives to offer works of art that are truly unique. The collectors who are drawn to this marketplace care about authenticity. Perhaps that's hinted at because it's secured by the Ethereum blockchain where NFTs originated. The actual works of art themselves are hosted on IPFs. On this blockchain, rarity is key.

Enjin Marketplace

When it comes to the notion of Ethereum being challenged for its place in NFT Marketplace history, the face it's usually given is Enjin Marketplace. Instead of utilizing Ethereum, Enjin has its own blockchain, and it encourages you to use its native currency, ENJIN COIN.

Gamers will rejoice because Enjin has a very strong game presence. Games such as *Multiverse, Age of Rust,* and *The Six Dragons* find a strong community here. True to the spirit of gaming, reward programs have gamified elements.

Portion

Portion puts across a refined and high-class image. It aims to directly connect artists and collectors together. There's a strong emphasis on complete transparency. They also aim to streamline selling, investing, and owning so that each stage is easy. In addition, Portion also make it possible to manage your physical and digital collection in one place.

By the time you have finished reading and applying everything that you are learning this book, there will surely have been more NFT marketplaces brought into existence. And they will all be grappling for dominance in their own individual niches.

Chapter 9: How do you create your own NFTs?

Hold it right there. I can see the twinkle in your eye. You want to dive headfirst into the NFT pool right *now!* Good for you. But before you start going fishing with hooks baited with diamonds, you're going to have to have a wallet for your NFTs and your profits to live in.

Not all crypto wallets are created equally. Just as there are a variety of blockchains, there are various wallets, and they aren't all compatible with each other or the marketplaces. Imagine the tragedy of minting an NFT that nets you several million dollars, but you don't have a digital wallet to receive the funds, or worse, you don't have a digital wallet that's compatible with the payment! Keep such nightmares from ever happening by doing your homework on wallets and matching up your needs.

All About Crypto Wallets

So what exactly is a cryptocurrency wallet? Is it electronic? Is it a piece of hardware? The truth is it can be both. Whichever route you go, one thing is certain. You cannot purchase and own

Bitcoin or any other cryptocurrency, including NFTs, without having some kind of cryptocurrency wallet. And you better make sure that your wallet is compatible with your NFT and the cryptocurrency you want to deal in or you'll have a payment that isn't collectible and essentially have given your NFT away.

It's interesting how much a crypto wallet has in common with a physical wallet. In your physical wallet, any paper money it contains represents the value that is in storage at the United States Treasury. So a crypto wallet also holds proof of your digital cash. It stores the public and private keys required to buy any cryptocurrency, including Bitcoin. It also provides digital signatures that authorize each transaction like a blockchain. As mentioned before, these wallets can take the form of an online app, a website, or a physical device that you can carry around with you. You would want to protect your keys the same way you would want to protect a password since those keys are what allow you to trade or spend your cryptocurrency.

Before moving forward, we should mention that an Ethereum wallet doesn't work exactly like a conventional physical wallet. Your crypto wallet does not actually store ether. It's actually not stored anywhere. Ether doesn't exist in any tangible shape or form. The only thing that exists are records on the blockchain, and your wallet contains the keys necessary to interact with the blockchain to enable transactions.

Let's suppose you decided to focus your NFT endeavors on where NFTs were born: the Ethereum blockchain. There are two main flavors of wallets—hot storage and cold storage.

Hot Storage

A hot storage wallet maintains a constant connection to the internet. The good news about this format is that you can easily access your funds from virtually anywhere in the world. But as history has proven time and time again, anything connected to the internet is vulnerable to theft. A determined hacker with no time limit can eventually find a way to steal your funds. Is it likely that this will happen? Who can say? But it is definitely possible.

Cold Wallet

Therefore, cold storage wallets store your keys offline and only connect to the internet when you want to. This is obviously a greater degree of security for your precious cryptocurrency.

Desktop Wallet

As the name implies, a desktop wallet is stored and runs on either your desktop computer or a laptop. You have options depending on how much storage space you have on your machine. You can download a full client with the entire blockchain or use a light client. Light clients are easier to use and store, but using a full client also has extra security since it doesn't rely on minors or nodes to pull accurate information. All the transactions are validated at the home base.

Desktop wallets aren't bad. They are convenient and relatively secure. You can only use them from the one computer where in which they were downloaded. But laptops and desktops are also connected to the internet, so it would be a good idea to spruce up on your cybersecurity measures. Make sure that the machine in question has not been hacked and is not infected by malware. And even more so, make sure that the computer in question is not at risk of being stolen.

Web Wallets

Web-based wallets have a number of things going for them. They're based on cloud storage technology which means that you can access them from pretty much anywhere in the world. They also clock a bit more speed than other kinds of crypto wallets. But in the eyes of many, a web wallet completely undermines the purpose of cryptocurrency. Since the wallet is stored online, that means that your keys are also stored online.

Don't forget that the cloud is a third-party server, which means the security of that server is completely out of your hands. The security of your funds and your keys rest squarely in the hands of whoever owns that server. That means that you are defenseless to take any measures against hackers, cyber-attacks, malicious malware, phishing scams, etc.

Hardware Wallets

If you just can't do without the familiarity of feeling a physical object in your pocket associated with your money, then there are hardware wallets. This is the ultimate cold storage method of cryptocurrency. They aren't unlike portable hard disks, except they are specifically made to work with cryptocurrency and blockchain technology. You can plug them into just about any computer when it's time to make a transaction. Better yet, key generation takes place offline. No hacker alive is going to be able to get past that.

Aside from that simple feature of being completely isolated from the reach of cyber-attacks, many hardware wallets come with backup security options to ensure that you won't lose your cryptocurrency. Many also provide the option of two-factor authentication as well as a password for an added level of security for your currency. There are now wallets on the market that also have a screen that allows you to sign for transactions on the device itself.

The extra security and peace of mind that comes with the hardware wallet also comes at a price. You will definitely lay down more money on a hardware wallet than you would on a software wallet. But if you're storing a large amount of cryptocurrency, then the investment will be more than worth it.

And like any device that was made for one singular function rather than a wide range of applications, hardware wallets weren't manufactured in massive quantities. So finding one for purchase might take a minute.

Custodial Wallets

Every so often, someone makes the news for losing their password or their security key to well over a billion dollars in cryptocurrency. The irony is almost too bitter to fathom since the wealth exists in storage, but the means of accessing it has literally evaporated from existence effectively separating its owner from the wealth.

A safeguard against this is utilizing a custodial wallet.

Again, some people see this as something that completely defeats the purpose of cryptocurrency. Since one of the whole points of crypto is to have complete control over your funds. A custodial wallet is a third-party service that offers storage and protection of your digital assets. So, if for some reason, you lost access to your funds because of some unforeseen loss with your keys or otherwise, you would be able to restore your ether from any other device.

Your security keys and your funds are both backed up by the provider's servers.

Minting Your NFTs

So it's time to bring a new NFT into the world. All of the marketplaces we just cited offer a page for minting a new NFT that is just as straightforward as uploading a picture to the internet and captioning it. The difference is that you're going to spend some crypto in the genesis of your new baby. But the actual creation of a new NFT is never rocket science. Whichever marketplace you do it in, you'll be walked through it step by step.

Chapter 10: What blockchain do you want your NFTs to live on?

Didn't we just get done with a really long list of places for your NFTs to be stored? That was a trick question. We got done with a long list of NFT marketplaces which is not the same as storage locations. The marketplaces are means by which you can display your NFTs and browse the works of others. Now it's time to look at how you will make it possible to pay for and receive payment for NFTs.

Choose wisely. Discrepancies in technology and plain old tribalism make it difficult, if not impossible, for some NFTs to be bought with certain cryptocurrencies. For example, there are no Bitcoin-based NFTs. At least not yet anyway.

Also, don't forget what part of the NFT lives on a blockchain. The token that gives the NFT its authenticity is what's stored on a blockchain, not the NFT itself. The information on the token points to the digital painting, video, or whatever the NFT happens to be. It's usually too expensive to store the NFT along with the token on the blockchain, so where the token lives and where the NFT itself is stored are typically two separate things.

Ethereum

It would be disrespectful to start this discussion with any blockchain other than Ethereum. Ethereum, after all, is where NFTs were born. Ethereum demonstrates staying power in the NFT sphere due to it being more than just a blockchain. It is also a solid development platform. Other blockchains trying to get a leg up on good old OG Ethereum are quick to point out that much of Ethereum's technology is outdated and doesn't handle scaling very well. Which is sadly true. The Ethereum blockchain is also still working out how to be more energy-efficient.

TechCrunch pointed out in a March 2021 article that each NFT transaction burns as much energy as two American households burn in a single day. Let that sink in for a moment. That's not just talking about buying and selling NFTs. That's buying and selling and minting. Two American households' daily energy consumption used up, just like that in one NFT transaction. And those expenses are forwarded to the users in the form of so-called gas prices, which are not cheap. For everything Ethereum has going for it as the starting point of the NFTs, it still has a few wrinkles to iron out that you will do well to consider.

Flow

Flow is one of the blockchains that have learned from Ethereum's mistakes. While Ethereum is a blockchain that just so happened to be hospitable to NFTs, Flow was specifically built with NFTs in mind, especially NFTs that concern games and collectibles. It's a dead giveaway considering that Flow was developed by *NBA Top Shot* developer, Dapper Labs.

Dapper Labs was paying attention when Ethereum was brought to a screeching halt by the buying and selling CryptoKitties, a collectible-driven NFT. So Flow was developed along with its own coin, the FLOW token.

Flow brags that its transactions are very fast and also low cost. There's also room for people who have an eye for development. Developers can create applications called dApps.

To put it in perspective, Flow is the equivalent of a PC that was specifically designed to run modern PC games, while other blockchains are like your uncle's clunky work computer that just might be able to pull off the odd game or two.

Wax

Wax is a clever acronym for Worldwide Asset eXchange.

Wax is even more focused on gaming than any of the other blockchains we've mentioned so far. It prides itself on being a carbon-neutral setup. It achieves this by running on a proof of stake system. And in their own words, they don't need supercomputers to wage an energy-sucking battle to complete a single transaction. It is a lean, green NFT mincing machine. That and the people behind Wax support reforestation.

There is room for most NFTs you can think of on Wax, but you're in especially good company if you're there to trade or sell items concerning video games and virtual worlds. Wax wants to cash in specifically on the massive video game industry. With 400 million players spending over $50 billion in virtual items annually, there's a lot of money for Wax to siphon off. Their premise is that if you purchase video game items outside of games, you'll be able to have items when you play that are truly unique and cannot be replaced or replicated when games are updated. This concept has been in development for a long time, ever since the trading and selling of items in *World of Warcraft* became a secondary market in 2004. So if you manage to craft an enchanted sword with special characteristics, you know where to sell it.

Tron

Every blockchain emphasizes decentralizing something. Tron wants to decentralize the internet. The setup that they have is well on its way to making that happen. Transaction speeds are very fast and much more reliable and scalable than Ethereum. While many blockchains are confined to the use of certain countries and nations, Tron is international, as are its users. They brag that their blockchain ecosystem allows users to freely publish, store, and own data. The Tron protocol is powered by the TRX coin.

Binance Smart Chain

Like Ethereum, Binance was not made with NFTs in mind. But it does a much better job of accommodating NFTs. Binance Smart Chain began showing off native NFTs in early 2021. People looking to take advantage of Binance Smart Chain will find a lively market for digital art, virtual pets, weapons, and items concerning games. And Binance Smart Chain users have the benefit of storing everything in the Trustwallet app.

EOS

This blockchain hasn't tightened its scope on NFTs like others have. They certainly do have the market space for NFTs, but they have a lot more on the table to offer. This blockchain is the sandbox of blockchains. Their primary focus is on developers who want to do anything with blockchain technology, whether NFTs, apps, or anything else. They describe themselves as a decentralized operating system. Their offer of processing transactions free of charge is difficult to look away from. The blockchain is open source and is powered by the EOS token.

Polkadot

Polkadot puts across a fun vibe as far as blockchains go. They don't really want to decentralize anything specifically, but they have stated that it is their mission to build bridges between multiple blockchains. That way, no matter which cryptocurrency you use or which blockchain you use to mint NFTs, you'll still be able to interact with one another and do business without loss of access to your NFT or currency. Polka dot also has a special aim toward staying viable no matter how technology or software changes. Polkadot operates with the DOT token.

Tezos

Tezos puts emphasis on its usefulness as a place to develop smart contracts. You'll never have to worry about Tezos falling into the wrong hands since the way things are set up places governance of the blockchain in the hands of its users. For whatever reason, Tezos has very high NFT engagement in all aspects of buying, selling, minting, and trading. Tezos is just as secure as Ethereum, but it uses a fraction of the energy processing NFTs. A big part of the energy behind the teaser's blockchain is the lively community. Much the way Dogecoin got its energy and vibe from its community, so it's the way with Tezos.

Cosmos

Cosmos takes the concept behind Polkadot's ambitions and projects it even bigger. Cosmos wants to be the internet of blockchains. Since each blockchain tends to be its own universe, closed to outside users of other systems, the cosmos wants to end the tribalism and bickering that is often fomented between different users of different blockchains.

For someone just getting into the NFT scene, the number of choices for cryptocurrencies and blockchains would seem to be overwhelming. But when it comes down to it, you don't need to overthink it. You just have to make sure that the people you're going to be doing business with, the cryptocurrency you prefer, the wallet you use, and the NFTs themselves are all compatible.

Chapter 11: Why is everyone investing in NFTs?

It almost seems like a question that shouldn't be asked. There are obviously millions of dollars to be had in the NFT craze in its current state. But there are actually more rational, rock-solid reasons why people are trying to get in on the whole NFT thing.

Part of it is understanding the mind of a collector. Collectors are drawn to scarcity. If something is genuinely one of a kind, then certain bragging rights come with owning it.

Just about any digital asset can be owned to an extent with a simple right click and save. But it's that originality that makes all the difference in the mind of a true collector.

You can take the $10 or $20 that you have in your pocket and go get a high-resolution poster of *Whistler's Mother* and frame it, and nobody would know the difference when they see it hanging in your home. And you might be perfectly satisfied with that. But the people who are truly collectors at heart would be kept awake at night by the simple fact that it's not the real *Whistler's Mother*. They would only be satisfied if they could own the real thing, the original. This is one of the biggest reasons collectors are willing to shell out mind-boggling amounts of money for a single work of art.

The connection to blockchain technology seals the appeal of an NFT. History is rife with people who have been swindled out of their hard-earned money because of an impeccably replicated masterpiece of work. Counterfeiting art has become an art unto itself, and as each new form of artwork becomes available, someone develops a way to copy it. So much so to the point that individual brush strokes are studied and replicated. Papers of authenticity and business transactions can easily be faked.

But under the advent of blockchain technology, where the ledger is automatically written and recorded and cannot be altered, the problem of counterfeit original art is solved, as long as a person doesn't mind that the asset is 100% digital.

Aside from collectors, there are concrete reasons why artists themselves are drawn to the NFT scene, and it's not just because they stand a chance at making a million dollars.

The problem of artists getting properly paid for their work is an issue as old as art itself. The speed and anonymity available on the internet have only exacerbated that problem for artists of all types.

The technology associated with buying and selling NFTs has proven to be a huge step in the right direction. Not only has blockchain technology allowed artists to control the connection of their credentials to a work of art, but it also solves some of the problems of the artists being properly paid for their work. It's all because of the technology of smart contracts that come with a transaction of an NFT.

The contracts are automated, and they ensure that each time an NFT is bought and sold, the artist makes a royalty off of it. There's no need for phone calls to be made and debts to be collected. When an artist's work changes hands in cyberspace, they get paid. Period. Boom. That would be like money getting deposited in DaVinci's bank account every time the *Mona Lisa* changed museums. Nobody would have to call him at his workshop in Italy. When the painting moves, money moves, and it goes to the right people.

Amongst the people who are dying to collect and those dying to sell, there are simply the people who don't have anything better to do. The pandemic has birthed a phenomenon referred to as recreational investing. When people are bored, they find ways of spending money. And the NFT scene is lighting up the map right now. Between Robinhood, cryptocurrency, and NFTs, this is the next logical stage of entertaining ways to spend your money.

Chapter 12: Are NFTs really a good investment?

No pun intended, but that really is the million-dollar question. The NFT scene right now is like a fire the moment that the flame catches and begins to swell.

Until recently, investing has always carried with it the unspoken rule of *Hey, we're doing this with an aim for the long term.* And what's clear about NFTs right now is that you can make money today.

What isn't clear is whether you will be able to make money with NFTs tomorrow.

The entire NFT sensation right now is very much like a wildfire as soon as it starts burning. Every fire starts out hot and bright. But the longevity of the fire depends entirely on what's fueling it and how solid and substantial it is. The only way to find out is to watch.

So what indicators are there right now that NFTs are a good investment? Are there any indicators that NFTs are a bad investment? Good or bad, there are definitely some things to keep an eye on when considering laying down your hard-earned cash on NFTs.

The front line of the NFT feeding frenzy is teeming with two kinds of people. Collectors and hagglers. Collectors are obviously looking to get one-of-a-kind items. And since NFTs have an indelible record from their birth, it's easy to understand why a collector would find them attractive. Hagglers are obviously trying to make a buck. And they surely will want to be able to make a buck later on down the road.

First, we'll look at NFTs from a money perspective. Whether you're collecting or trying to make a dollar, it would be nice to think that at some point, you could unpack all of your valuable million-dollar NFTs and turn them around for some quick cash if you needed to. The profitability of NFTs right now relies on the newness of the market. The NFT world is very much an unregulated Wild West. It's fueled by the freedom of a world that is uncertain about how these things should be regulated. Right now, if you have access to the internet, a blockchain, and you can set up a digital wallet, you can mint your own NFTs, and you can put them up for sale on a number of outlets.

As of this writing, authority figures worldwide are looking at ways of leveling regulations against Bitcoin. Granted, NFTs have very little to do with Bitcoin and are more Ethereum based. But if regulations eventually go through for one cryptocurrency, it's only a matter of time before they go through for the rest.

If the world's fat cats have their way and manage to find ways of regulating cryptocurrency, how will that affect people's ability to freely whip out their digital wallets and drop as much money as they want on an NFT? NFTs currently cost their owner so much just to keep them alive in storage. The movement of information on a blockchain and the upkeep associated with keeping the blockchain accurate all add up to gas prices. This means that each time an NFT is moved around or sold, some charges are accrued. This is done so mostly by the cost in energy and electricity that it takes to store and move information on the blockchain.

While it is possible to turn some respectable money if you're selling NFTs, your NFTs will slowly draw money out of your wallet until you make those sales.

And then some NFTs hold no value at all. While it's true that it's not possible to counterfeit an NFT work of art, it is possible to push a work of digital art by an artist who isn't that high profile as if it's the next best thing that should be in your collection. People eager to get in on the NFT craze are not always stopping to think before they buy and check out exactly where this NFT originated and if the person who made it is going to be worth that much money either tomorrow or in the near future. Consequently, honest businesspeople trying to play the game correctly are getting swindled out of their money. The fact that you're reading this book shows that you probably have some gaps in your knowledge about NFTs, which means you're susceptible to such swindling on some level if you're not careful. All it will take is a solid sales pitch and some gaps in your research to get you to part with your hard-earned money, and you're left with an NFT that isn't going to be worth anything—ever.

Others are afraid that at some point, governments will figure out a way to tax cryptocurrency.

An additional issue is the nature of the NFT itself. If you were a collector of actual physical works of art, and the money for them just wasn't on the market at the time, you would simply put them back in storage and wait till the prices in the market were more favorable. As long as you've got a warehouse with a sturdy gate and a solid lock, you don't have anything to worry about, minus tornadoes and hurricanes, but even then, you can insurance tangible assets.

Since NFTs are intangible, they are subject to a whole host of incidental factors that could wipe them out from existence in a second.

Anybody who's been using a computer for more than a year discovers that technology never stays the same. There will always be an update. There will always be a new release. Somebody finds a way to reinvent the entire thing over again, so operating systems and file storage technology become obsolete in relatively short periods. The current technology behind the blockchain may be state of the art right now, but inevitably, it will advance, and it will change.

Programs and games that ran fine on Windows 98 and Windows XP will not run and cannot be played on Windows 10, not without extensive workarounds.

It could be that advances in technology and updates could render an NFT either unviewable, unusable, or even erase it from existence. Even if NFT technology and blockchain technology more or less stay the same, there are always security risks. Once in a while, the news will publish a story on people with well over a billion dollars in cryptocurrency in their wallet, but because they lost their digital key and didn't plan for any kind of backup, their fortune is irretrievable. Not by them, not by anyone.

Some people take every possible step to preserve their digital goods, and even all those measures can be trumped by the fact that there's always a glitch. Now you might not be planning on hanging on to any NFT long enough for these kinds of problems to develop. That doesn't mean that there aren't any problems that threaten your digital assets right now.

The only thing that the blockchain promises to store is the token associated with the NFT. When it comes down to it, that's what you truly have ownership of when you make a purchase of an NFT. Without the token, the NFT is nothing. The token lives on the blockchain and is sustained by the peer-to-peer network of computers that keep it accurate and alive. The digital work of art? For it to exist, it has to be either stored on a local hard drive, or it has to be hosted by a provider.

When web hosting bills don't get paid, providers start shutting people off, and that unpaid bill could spell the end of your million-dollar NFT storage. Okay, fine, suppose you have a reliable provider, and you have more than enough money to pay the hosting fees. Guess what? Businesses and companies still get bought out. Which could change the technology that's used to host. Which, again, could threaten your NFT.

Even in a perfectly fail-safe scenario, there's always the wild card factor of the government stepping in and shutting down a website or a service due to alleged copyright infringements. And when they step in, they don't just shut down part of the site. They shut down the whole thing. If that's where your NFT has been stored, it gets locked down along with everything else. If you do the smart thing and make it a point to back up your NFT by storing it locally, then the only thing you have to worry about is the longevity and the physical safety of the equipment you use for storage.

All of this might have sounded like a lot to take in. Should any of these factors discourage you from investing in NFTs? Not necessarily. If you're going to invest in valuable things, you have to learn how to take care of them and find out what can ruin them or spoil them. It's the same with people who spend thousands of dollars on a rare or fine wine. It's not that you shouldn't lay down the money for it; however, it would just be smart to find out how to properly care for it and store it.

Some say that the NFT craze is just a bubble, and it's eventually going to pop. When the internet was brand new, the craze of e-commerce that it set off was a bubble as well. The bubble has long since popped, and guess what? The internet is still with us. Internet-based business is still with us, and it's more streamlined and more sophisticated than ever before. The pop of the internet bubble didn't destroy the internet. It just blew away all the crap and hype that got in the way of the legit, solid stuff.

Right now, the NFT craze is fueled by a lot of good and legitimate business and also a lot of bad, hokey business. When the bubble pops, and if the bubble pops, the landscape of NFTs will be vastly different.

Something as simple as a broken link could deny you access to a million-dollar NFT. How so? It typically is too expensive to store a digital image on the token itself on the blockchain. So the information on the token will point to where the digital image or NFT is stored. Pointing to that NFT requires the use of a URL. If that URL is broken, then access to the NFT is broken.

Then there are the potential risks posed by cloud storage itself. Cloud storage is marketed as this abstract way of storing your precious data in this lofty place in the sky where it'll be forever safe and secure.

Don't forget that cloud storage is actually a warehouse full of servers and hard drives—a physical entity you've stored all your precious things on. These things are nowhere near being found in the sky; instead, they are very much land-bound. Anything on land is subject to the hazards of the rest of us anchored on terra firma. With natural disasters on the rise, the improbable but not impossible demise of any and all servers that store your digital investments is not something to be dismissed lightly. The odds would be like winning the lottery in a bad way. But people can and do win the lottery regularly.

Cryptocurrency is also coming under fire for how much raw energy it requires to create new tokens and store them. This energy consumption is significant. Otherwise, holders of cryptocurrency wouldn't pay small fees constantly.

If you have a soft spot in your heart for the footprint that mankind leaves on the natural world, then the energy consumed by NFT business will get your attention. If it doesn't, it's only a matter of time before it significantly gets the attention of the authorities. A big part of the profitability of the NFTs right now is because nobody knows how to regulate them. But as with all things, that will change at some point. The government will likely find a way to step in to regulate and tax it to take its fair share.

At the end of the day, NFTs are worth whatever people are willing to pay for them, just like any other collectible. NFTs could very well be a joke, but right now, it's a million-dollar joke. Just make sure that you don't end up being the punchline.

Chapter 13: Investing and making money with NFTs

More than likely, you're going to devote the bulk of your investments to NFT artwork. That's what this section will focus on, but bear in mind that the principles apply to other NFTs you might want to invest in as well.

Investing in NFTs is very similar to investing in the stock market. You buy low, and you sell high. You speculate on the future of a company or a stock, and you try to get on board with them while they're still small and obscure so that you can turn around and make a profit when they're much bigger and more popular.

NFT artwork functions much the same way, except it carries more of a personal touch. If you're going to invest in NFT art, prepare to find yourself getting emotionally invested on a personal level to some extent. Don't worry, this will be a good thing. Because when an artist detects that you're emotionally invested in their work, it will bolster them to perform their best and put some momentum behind your financial and emotional investment in their craft.

This will call on you to look at NFT art with both a logical and an emotional eye. Artwork that is clearly provocative, bold, and ostensibly unique will make a splash of some kind of some size. It's just a matter of how big and when.

If you're one of the first people to be discovering this artist, all the better. That means that you have first grabs at their work. You'll be paying less than you would be paying for anybody else who's already garnering attention, but you're trusting in your instincts and even more to see where their future is headed. It cannot be overstated that being one of the people who makes those first investments in an artist's work motivates them to keep trying and keep going. Your investment makes a difference to artists in particular.

Now, if you've come across an artist who's already starting to gain some traction, then it's an even safer bet that their artwork is going to be a good investment later on down the road. But obviously, you're going to be paying higher prices to get in on their work.

There are indeed many aspects of business that are cold and impersonal, but to the extent that you can, try to form an attachment to specific artists you're hoping will blow up. The perception of fandom or a relationship will be perceptible on their end. When you can leave comments on their work, go ahead and do so. When you can upvote their work, do it. All these seemingly meaningless actions are the things that metaphorically water them and make them grow, which will make them turn out higher-quality artwork faster. You'll benefit in the end from a harvest of profits. Speaking of which...

Once you perceive that the market is ripe for a higher price on the artwork you bought, it's a simple matter of flipping the NFT and making a profit on it. The earning potential for digital art is astronomical. But at its core, the mechanic is similar to flipping antiques.

If you manage to successfully sell an artist's work, that too will encourage the artist that you've chosen to focus on, especially if the NFT has any smart contracts attached to it. Thanks to smart contracts, the artist will make a percentage of the sales when it changes hands again. It's motivating to the artist when you buy the artwork. But it's all so motivating when you manage to sell the artwork for a higher price and get the artist a profit they weren't counting on.

The same principles apply to other NFT assets, such as digital sports cards. If a new celebrity or a new athlete comes on the scene and they seem to have potential, you want to snatch up any official NFTs related to them before they blow up.

Another arena of NFT profitability, not to be overlooked, is purchasing domain names as NFTs. Especially names that could be derived from the ENS or Ethereum Name Service. A vanilla Ethereum address is a really long number that's impossible to memorize, and the sting is taken out of this by using the Ethereum Name Service. A similar mechanic is behind the reason you can just type in google.com and be taken there instead of typing out the really long, native address where Google is truly reached. The more unique the name, the more you're going to pay for it but also the more you can turn around and sell it for. This is tricky and will involve some critical judgment on your part to guesstimate what sort of names of addresses could be highly valuable later on down the road.

Chapter 14: Can you become a millionaire investing in NFTs?

Yes, you *can* become a millionaire investing in NFTs.

But that's not what you came here to hear, is it? You don't want to hear about the possibility. You want something certain. You want a concrete promise that you will be putting away a million dollars into your bank account at some point.

Well, I'm glad you bought this book and no other. Because any book that promises you a million dollars is a book that has pretty much stolen your money.

I will tell you that you may become a millionaire through NFTs. I will tell you that it's likely you will become a millionaire through NFTs. But I'm not going to promise you that you'll be a millionaire through NFTs because nobody can make that promise and keep it.

Something that's been stated throughout this book more than once is that the NFT market is so profitable right now because of how new it is. Nobody knows how to regulate it. The governments don't know how to tax it. So it's very much like the California Gold Rush.

The NFT market is going to change dramatically at some point. Maybe for better, maybe for worse. But change it will. It could change under the weight of laws and regulations. It could change under the weight of advances in software and technology. Nevertheless, it will change.

But as long as authenticity, scarcity, and uniqueness are valuable to collectors, NFTs will always have a considerable dollar amount attached. Maybe the profit ceiling will remain in the millions. Maybe it will lower over time. But with persistence and determination and getting to know the psychology of the market, you'll always be able to turn a dollar with NFTs.

A bigger question than "Can I make a million dollars on NFTs?" is if you can lose a million dollars on NFTs. I'm not trying to discourage you from getting into the scene by any means. But some aspects of the NFT market are like a minefield. And anything you can do to tell where the mines are, the better off you'll be.

The worth of an NFT, especially when it comes to digital artworks, is often based on inflated social media concepts of reputation. Human beings are turned into memes, and they become celebrities overnight. Then somebody does some digging, and they find some discrepancy in the overnight celebrity's life. And just as quickly as the world fell in love with him, the world vilifies them.

The point is that the value placed on these people and what they make and do is wildly subject to change. In the age of the internet, sometimes these changes come about overnight.

And that's what happens in the case of honest chance and circumstance. We haven't even touched on the people looking to take advantage of and fleece the people who are new to the NFT market.

Some legitimate NFTs that have commanded prices in the millions don't exactly look like fine art. CryptoKitties and CryptoPunks immediately come to mind.

That said, any digital image that could even remotely be called art can be minted into an NFT and pitched with a hard sell as a work of genius produced by an up-and-coming, hot artist whose work will be worth millions in the near future. The digital token attached to the image will show you who minted it and who, if anyone, has owned it before, but it doesn't tell you if the sales pitch is accurate or not.

Right now, conditions are ripe for making relatively easy money from NFTs.

High-profile digital artists have dealt with issues including identity theft, where people set up camp on NFT marketplaces, pretending to be them and minting their artwork into NFTs without the original user's permission.

It's one thing to have your art minted and sold without your permission, but it's entirely another thing for someone else to be claiming to be you.

It has become routine for some artists to check major NFT marketplaces to ensure they aren't being impersonated and their artwork isn't being minted and sold without their say.

And don't forget that once an NFT is created, legitimately or not, it lives on that blockchain forever.

But for all the potential pitfalls of NFTs, the possibility of making a million dollars and beyond is very real.

I would encourage you to experience the satisfaction of several breakthroughs before aiming for the moon and being disappointed if you fall flat.

First, try to see if you can get an NFT to sell for a few hundred dollars. Then see if you can get several NFTs to sell for the same price. Build confidence in the process and in the market before you start taking on big numbers like millions. Those sales might not be putting you in the country club, but they will certainly pay the bills, and they will afford you time to build your own confidence in yourself and your own business intuition and also build an online reputation.

Even if you don't make a million dollars, the average prices garnered by NFTs are still relatively high.

As of this writing, the average sale price on SuperRare is $5,800, the average price on Maker'sPlace is $2,400, and the average on Foundation is $3,500. It may not be a million, but that's still good money for the effort involved.

And don't overlook the classic formula of high-volume goods at low prices. If you're turning out impressive NFTs that are hundreds if not thousands of dollars cheaper than all the other sellers, you won't have to worry about sales.

Chapter 15: How do you buy NFTs?

Have you ever bought anything over eBay before? If so, good. You're already primed for most of the ways that buying NFTs works. If you haven't used eBay before, don't worry. The business end of the NFT-scape is simpler than it sounds.

Similar to eBay, many NFT marketplaces function like an auction. After you place a bid, you sit back and wait to see if you won.

Also, like eBay, some NFT marketplaces allow you the option of buying right away instead of sitting back and bidding, and you can get what you want at a fixed price.

Something you'll eventually catch on to is not every cryptocurrency is owned in whole tokens by people who go buying NFTs. So you'll find that the prices of NFTs are usually listed in decimals of the currency being used. This is often accompanied by a dollar value, too. But the dollar value can change often because of the volatility of the cryptocurrency trading price. The prices of cryptocurrency never hold still, but it will give you an estimate of what you're actually paying for the NFT.

You'll also be paying a gas fee, this is an expense that fluctuates, and it's money that goes to the miners who supply the computing power for the blockchain. Some blockchains have found other ways of financing this, and the burden is taken off of users.

In any case, you will need to have set up a digital wallet, and you will have to have purchased some cryptocurrency to spend on the NFTs. Some platforms allow you to purchase crypto using a credit card. This includes Coinbase, Kraken, Etoro, and even PayPal and Robinhood. From there, you move the currency from the exchange to your wallet.

Chapter 16: What is the cheapest place to buy NFTs?

There is no designated official space for thrift shop NFTs. Often the bargains will be found with creators who are just coming onto the scene and are trying to get a foothold.

If you feel that the maker or what they're producing has a bigger future, then you could take advantage of their small beginnings and their NFTs and wait to see if their value increases over time. If the name of the creator gets bigger or the hype and popularity surrounding the kind of NFT they create increases, then you'll be able to turn around and make a profit on whatever you bought.

You'll find that you'll have to develop a sort of business intuition that is not unlike the intuition developed by someone who plays the stock market. There's a certain knack to looking at a certain asset or good and being able to accurately guess if they're going to blow up in the future. Otherwise, you'll end up with an entire database of NFTs that are worth no more than they were when you bought them.

You can offset this formula a little bit by placing your money on NFTs that already carry some value, which could call for more. Digital sports cards come to mind. The sports arena is already full of celebrities who are each worth quite a bit of money in whatever form they are marketed—digital, physical, or otherwise. Which will call on you sometimes to lay down money that's anything but affordable for the average person.

It will be critical for you to set aside a fund dedicated to investing in NFTs, and it will be even more critical for you to carefully evaluate which NFTs are worth your time.

It might be more worth your time to ask questions like, "Where can I get more money without working two full-time jobs so that it doesn't take twelve years for me to have enough extra cash to invest in NFTs?"

Where Can I Get More Money to Invest in NFTs?

Investing in general, not just investing in NFTs, calls on the would-be investor to find a way to build a pool of money to invest and a steady income to keep that pool from running dry. That said, be prepared to play the long game if you're serious about making NFTs a major part of your investing game.

Specific side hustles aside (which we'll address immediately after this part), the process goes as follows.

#1. Learn a new, high-paying skill

Congratulations. You're living in 2021. You can pick up and learn about a plethora of skills for free through YouTube, Pinterest, and just plain ol' Google searches. The free route might take some extra time and more than the usual confidence in your ability to learn without an instructor, but it is possible. If you'd rather save time, you can always find a home study course, or go the traditional route and enlist in a face-to-face program.

#2. Start making money with that new skill

Once you know enough to start making money, do it. Learning is good and well, but there's no substitute for real-world practice. Build your confidence in your new skill by getting results (and money) from exercising it. Even if you don't make much, you need that actual practice as soon as possible.

#3. Become the best you possibly can at that skill

Once you're finally holding real money in your hands that you earned from your new skill, then you need to take things a step further. Learn more about your skill. Level up by deepening your knowledge. Branch out and acquire associated skills. As far as you can, become the absolute best. Become so good at it that you could teach somebody else if you wanted to or had to. By now, you're probably dying to start putting some money into your NFT investment fund. Which you can do. But don't get frustrated if that extra money is just a trickle for the time being. The time that you're investing in your new skill and scaling it up is going to be worth it. To find out why, read the very next section.

#4. Diversify your execution of that skill

Here's where all your hard work finally pays off. Now that you are an expert in your new skill, you can find different ways of making money with it so that you have multiple streams of income. Besides doing the work on behalf of others, now you can put together an online or home study course that you teach yourself.

Depending on how you go about putting that course out to the world, some services will pay you for the course without any extra tutorship from you. In addition to that, now you can write a book about your field and put your own unique spin on the information.

The basics of any field indeed stay the same, but what's truly unique and priceless is the individual experience. No two journeys in a skill are the same, which means that your book will have something special to offer. And I don't think you have to write a novel's length worth of words and how to. In this day and age, you can find books on Amazon, Smashword, and beyond that are 20,000, 10,000, and 5,000 words. You could write multiple books on the same subject and develop several sources of income that way.

If people start seeking you out for one-on-one consultation or coaching, make it a point to charge a premium for your time.

High-paying skills that can easily be leveraged for NFT money

Social Media Manager

One of the ironies of small businesses is that as much control as you have over how things operate, you might have minimal time or control over your ability to promote your own business. A lot of effort goes into developing content, where to share it, how to optimize it, and how to measure the metrics of its successful. Then there's also the need to follow up on all the generated leads and massage those leads into sales.

Content campaigns are written up weeks, if not months in advance. This is all very time-consuming for someone who's at the helm of the business. This means there's lots of room for people like you if you have the savvy to write content that converts sales and post it on social media. Many business owners will pay good money to have a social media manager grow their business and their sales for them to focus on the day-to-day operations of keeping their business going.

This is both an easy and lucrative way to build funds for your NFT habits.

Etsy Seller

If you're already a digital artist, then you've heard of Etsy at least once. And you might be overlooking its potential of getting your feet wet in investing. Granted, it does take some time to get noticed, but once you gain traction, you can have at least a little bit of dependable and disposable income. It may not be available as a day job, but it can be useful as a side hustle for your NFT investment ambitions.

This may require you to wear the sales hat, and if that's something you're not used to, it may be uncomfortable at first. But it depends on how serious you are about making this pursuit viable.

There are entire communities devoted to marketing yourself and gaining traction on Etsy. As far as opinions go, this writer believes there are faster and more profitable ways of starting a side hustle. But if you are a capable artist and a capable salesperson, you will be able to make this work.

Freelance Copywriter

Copywriting has been one of the best-kept secrets of the writing world as far as how easy it is to break into and how much money you can make from it. Even people with an average ability to write can become successful copywriters. Fifty dollars an hour is considered cheap for copywriting. In our era of information being available everywhere, if you have persistence, grit, and self-confidence, you can teach yourself to become a copywriter and get started through information available on YouTube, Pinterest, and various PDFs on the subject scattered around the internet.

One of the ways the copywriters make money is by hooking people who want to learn to copywrite and hook you and make a lot of valuable information available for free of charge. The information that's available for free of charge is plenty to get you started. It might not be enough to get you earning fifty dollars an hour off the bat, but it's enough for you to start getting your foot in the door and earning some side income.

The reason why more people aren't copywriters is that the material being written isn't exactly thrilling. Where ghostwriters might have the entertaining experience of writing novels, copywriters write all the boring stuff that nobody else wants to write. Sales letters. Sales emails. Blogs. Advertisements. Junk mail. All the stuff that's not likely to tap into your sense of adventure, but this is where the big earnings truly are in the writing world. With freelancer marketplaces like Upwork and Fiverr, it's easier than ever before to get your foot in the door and start running quickly.

When you want to upgrade your earning potential, train yourself on specific areas of copywriting through resources like LinkedIn learning, home study courses, or, again, YouTube. Ask permission from each client to use completed projects as portfolio pieces. If you don't have any portfolio pieces for a particular area that you want to break into, do your best to create a mock-up of one for a fictional company. This is not being dishonest. Good writing is good writing, whether it's been done for a real company or not. It demonstrates the validity of what you can do.

A slight tongue-in-cheek warning for this particular side hustle. You might be so absorbed in the money that you can make from copywriting, you might be distracted from the money you can make investing in NFTs. But only NFTs have the potential to make you a million dollars in a short amount of time.

Podcast Editing

If you've never produced a podcast, then you might not appreciate just how much polishing goes into the final product. It's more than just editing out flubs and word whiskers. It's also tightening up the sound quality, editing out breaths and distracting noises in the background. The recording process in the studio can be time-consuming. It's even more time-consuming to deliver a podcast with no distracting elements and it sounds like everything went perfectly on the first take.

That's another thing; a podcast usually consists of several takes that are condensed down into one post-production. Many high-profile podcasters also want an accurate transcript to accommodate the podcast in the show notes. Relatively few podcasters can make a sustainable living from their podcast, so it's normally just a side hobby that they do for their soul food, or they're trying to massage it into a day job. They're probably struggling to balance the normal responsibilities of life plus creating a podcast, let alone making it perfect. If you have editing skills and you're able to work with a digital audio workstation, there is a steady flow of side income for you to make the big bonuses that podcasters want to keep show going, so if you do go to work for them, you'll have an ongoing supply of work with each new episode.

Podcasting

You can always turn the above recommendation inside out. You can be the podcaster yourself. You'll have to figure out how you're going to manage the editing process as discussed above, but if you do and if your podcast gains the audience, then you can make decent money by selling out ad space at the beginning, end, or mid-roll of your show. The more reach your podcast gets, the more money you make from each advertisement.

The beauty of living in 2021 is that podcast hosting services offer you a completely free package with the option to monetize your podcast right out the door from your first episode. Anchor.FM is one of these. They've made the effort to give you everything you need to produce a decent podcast in the mobile app or on the online web application. They recommend ads for you to use at any point in your show; you record them yourself and place them where you see fit.

Take notice that it's not an instant goldmine. Your show will need to have a considerable reach before you make a significant amount of money to divert into your NFT investment ambitions. But for a service that lets you monetize your podcast from episode one, the prospect is very attractive.

Blogging

One might think that the world of blogging has reached a point of saturation by now as the number of blogs has numbered into the millions. But just as blogs have grown, so have readers. So there's still money to be made in the blogging field. There are just as many subjects to write about as ever, and people are willing to read what you write. Blogging, in particular, has a long baking time; that is, it will likely take a long time for you to gain the readership that you need to be able to start monetizing your blog. But there are so many ways to get yourself there faster, especially if you blog in conjunction with producing a podcast which is one of the suggestions in this list.

Many transcripts of podcasts will do just fine as a blog post. So blogging and podcasting go hand in hand. Once you're able to monetize your blog, the income you earn from it is almost passive. Almost. You might even be able to successfully blog about NFTs.

If you chronicle your journey into investing and monetizing NFTs and you become successful, documenting your journey will be valuable to others trying to get into the same scene. And right now, there's so much money going into the NFT craze that you won't have to worry about anyone measuring up as substantial competition.

Author

The best time to make money from writing books is now. Authors and writers are no longer at the mercy of big publishing houses, which used to have the say-so whether a book made it or not. This will call on you to pick up extra skills such as knowing how to self-publish and market your book, but the time from conception to sales for a book has been shortened dramatically because of how much power has been placed in the hands of the author.

Whether you want to write the next up-and-coming thriller novel or whether you're going to pen a book on how to cash in on the NFT craze like this one, the odds of you making good money from a book is higher than it's ever been before. The only catch is that it's still a numbers game. If you want to make substantial money from books, you have to write a substantial number of books. Plus, you have to produce books in a timely enough manner to cash in on people's interests while they're still interested.

Your success may also depend on your ability to write about things you may not necessarily be interested in. For example, if you want to make it big as a fiction writer, romance is hotter than it's ever been before. But you might not be particularly fond of romance, let alone writing it. But if you can get yourself to write in the genre, you can guarantee yourself steady work.

Mystery Shopper

How do grocery stores and other establishments find out how their people are really doing? They hire mystery shoppers. Employees are really good at putting on a good front when authority figures are watching. The mystery shopper finds out how things are truly being done when the manager isn't walking the floor.

This hidden performance of a company's people is valuable information, and companies are willing to pay for it. Some apps allow you to be a general mystery shopper across a wide variety of industries, such as Field Agent. But keep in mind that this is one of the lowest-paying gigs on this list. There are mystery shoppers who make good money. But it isn't always steady work, and the high-paying gigs are almost not worth the time it takes to find them. But it depends on your skillset and the time and money you're willing to invest in NFTs.

Ghostwriter

There are people who have a book inside of them, but they're either too busy or too uncertain about their writing ability to get it done.

If you can demonstrate an ability to turn people's thoughts and ideas into words on a page, you could build a career as a ghostwriter. Ghostwriters write everything from memoirs to nonfiction books, blog posts, and even smaller, simpler projects like essays.

The reason that more people are not ghostwriters is because of what happens once the project is completed. If you agreed to write a series of romance novels as a ghostwriter, once the project is completed, you take no credit for the finished product, and you do not make a royalty on sales. You're paid a fee for your services, and your client's name takes all the credit for the work. This is perfectly legal, but it doesn't sit well with some people.

But if you're looking for money to put into NFTs so you can eventually make a million dollars, it shouldn't matter that much.

The world is ripe with good-paying ghostwriting projects if you figure out where to look and if you build your credentials. After all, what's a byline on a series of novels compared to a million dollars?

Ghostwriting used to be an industry that you had to know people to break into. Now it's as simple as perusing job boards for ghostwriters found on Facebook, Reddit, and similar community built places. The most reliable ghostwriting gigs are found in high-profile marketplaces like Fiverr and Upwork.

If this sounds like a really long way of doing things, you're right. It is. But this is also how it's done in other forms of investing. People who want to start investing in real estate, the stock market, or anything else, find a way of getting a steady flow of income so that they can keep investing instead of investing in just a few places.

A consistent cash pool will go much further than just a handful of dollars that you try to invest at the "right" times.

By the time you master one of these skills and start generating income from it, you might think there's no longer any point in putting money into NFTs. And for you, that might be true. It all depends on the value you place on your earnings potential in the NFT market.

One of these skills could keep you in good earnings as either a side hustle or full-time pursuit. But remember why you started the NFT journey in the first place. You want to make a million dollars, right?

At the very least, if for some reason it turns out that it's no longer possible to make that big million in the NFT industry, you've picked up and perfected a skill that has much more earning potential than whatever nine-to-five you currently hold. And, of course, there's plenty of other things to invest your money in besides NFTs. It's just that the NFT market is what's especially hot right now.

Chapter 17: What are some of the best NFTs to invest in right now?

This fluctuates often, but right now, these are the top contenders.

Digital Art

Sports Cards

Collectibles

Domain Names

Chapter 18: How do you monetize digital art NFTs?

This section will be especially useful to artists trying to get their foot in the door in the NFT world.

Past sections have already shown how to mint your work of art into a token that has nothing like it anywhere else in the world. But how do you get people to fork over that high-dollar amount that NFTs carry?

The approach is very similar to any other art market. You need a niche, and you need to find an audience for that niche. The more you look around NFT marketplaces, the more you'll notice that they are not all created equally. Different tribes of people congregate in different marketplaces. So, once you've decided on the kind of artwork you want to make, you need to determine which marketplace is most likely to have the people who would fall in love with what you produce.

One of the trademarks of NFTs is scarcity. You're going to have to decide if the works you produce will be runs of series or if they're going to be standalone. Because some marketplaces are only open to one kind. Some collectors turn their noses up at a painting if it's part of a series but would buy the exact same thing if it was the only one of its kind. Paintings that run in a series or a limited edition are easier and faster to produce but don't have the same branding of scarcity as paintings that are one of a kind. You'll have to think about this before you start cranking out your NFTs.

Chapter 19: Do I have to be a famous artist to use NFTs?

No, you don't. And you don't even have to be talented.

I'll wait for you to recover from that statement. Ready for more? Good.

If you're reading this section, I'm going to make the assumption that you're an artist. Perhaps you're making a move to digital to cash in on the NFT scene, or perhaps you're a digital artist already, and you're looking to make a move to some blockchain-fueled profits.

It is my honest wish that you succeed in your endeavors. I truly do hope that you have what you need to get out there by the time you're done reading this book and start dropping some works of art that win over payments that could be considered works of art.

But just in case things don't go that way for you, this section has been specially designed to help you pursue profits from artwork no matter what the NFT scene does.

How well are your paintings selling right now? Have you sold any paintings at all? If the answer is no, that's okay.

It's time to teach you how to be a successful artist with or without the help of NFTs. Hopefully with. But if the NFT craze were to burn out by tomorrow morning when you open your eyes, I want you to still be able to turn a dollar from your artwork, be it digital, traditional, or otherwise.

You'll find that what holds true in selling NFT works of art holds true in selling any other kind of art in any market.

You've likely noticed that there are a lot of artists who make a lot of money, but they don't seem to be that talented. You can wave it away with the explanation that they found their niche or they found their audience, but that's only a small part of it. The bigger part of it is the same reason that mediocre pop stars can sell multi-platinum records with minimal talent and zero songwriting skills. They do this while the genuine musical artists are playing in bars on the weekends and not getting signed to any big contracts. What is that bigger part? It's clearly not talent. Because if it were a question of talent, the devoted musicians who play in the bars at a loss would be where the pop stars are.

That bigger part, my friend, is reach. When the bigshots in the world's entertainment machine discover a new pop star, they take what little talent they might have and broadcast it far and wide. Then it becomes a game of averages. Yeah, only one in fifty people like Peter Pop Star's new hit single, but when broadcasting and advertising is putting his music in millions of ears a day, it doesn't matter how many people don't like his music. The people that do still fork over a very nice profit.

As a visual artist, your reach is more than just getting your work into a gallery or into an online marketplace to sell as an NFT. Your reach is principally how much you produce and how quickly. You will build more profit and more reach by doing twenty paintings in a week that aren't your best, but they're still good as opposed to doing five paintings in a week that are your absolute best and you obsess over every detail. Each completed work of art represents an exponential number of eyes that could be exposed to your work.

If you're an obscure artist, your focus should be to create, create, create. Create a huge volume of work that's good but not necessarily your best. If you make a hundred paintings that appeal to two out of five people who see them, you're going to sell more paintings than you would if you only created ten paintings that appeal to four out of every five people who see them.

The trick is to produce these works as affordably as possible. And since NFT works of art are 100% digital, the only real expense will probably be the electricity it takes to run your tablet and your computer. So once you figure out how to be prolific, you're sitting on a gold mine.

By the time you're reading this sentence, I trust that several weeks or months have passed, and you've produced a huge amount of digital works of art.

It's going to be tempting to jump into the NFT scene headlong and mint each work of art into an NFT. But don't forget that each NFT will cost you to keep it alive. Gas prices, remember? So consider making prints of your works or offering them on print-on-demand websites to build some traction underneath your name since this is more affordable.

But if you're absolutely dying to mint some NFTs, go right ahead.

If you sense that you're starting to build a following, then your time to cash in is getting close. You'll want to keep the work coming as usual, but you'll also want to produce some works that are labeled as a special edition, or especially rare, or as one of a kind, never to be repeated. Tighten the scarcity window even further by offering some items for sale for only twenty-four hours or even shorter.

Find a good price range that's much cheaper than the other artist gaining traction but enough that you don't do so at a loss due to gas prices or other expenses.

This is an industry secret that many people in a variety of artistic pursuits will overlook. They think that if they don't make it big, it has something to do with their talent. Talent could be a factor, but it's not the main issue. The main issue is reach and exposure, and the fastest way to exposure and reach is by being prolific.

Understand this and master this, and nothing will stop you. Have days in the studio or at the desk or wherever you produce your art, or you try to find out how many paintings you can turn out in a short period of time. Once you've established a daily record, strive to tighten up your process so that you can turn out even more. To the best of your ability, flood your market. The more soldiers you have on the battlefield, the more likely you are to win this war.

<u>Chapter 20: Can you rely on NFTs as a long-term investment?</u>

Well, looking back on all the history of NFTs, the data shows… Oh, wait. There isn't any data. There's no long-term record of the market for NFTs. It's like asking for data on the California Gold Rush while it was happening. Nobody knew what the price of gold was going to be after all this gold would be put on the market and into circulation. The phenomenon was simply too young to determine anything about the future.

The only thing people understood was in the present. That if you rolled up your sleeves and you got to work right away, and you worked as hard and as long as possible, you stood a high chance of coming out with some really good profits. The NFT phenomenon is at that stage right now. It's brand new. It's way too young to forecast what it is going to be like in the future. So everything we know about it is what's happening right now. But if you get to work and get moving, you stand a good chance of tidying up your profits.

The NFTs that you hold onto, what are they going to be worth in the future? We're going to have to get to the future to find out. Nobody knows right now, but that hasn't stopped people from speculating about what's coming. Not surprisingly, there are just as many bulls as there are bears. Here are a few perspectives.

Samson Mow is the Chief Strategy Officer at Blockstream. He explained that part of the NFT explosion is a lot of hype. Hype doesn't last forever. While the hype is here, it has driven many companies and individuals to mint NFTs as quickly as possible. The vast majority of these NFTs were highly experimental. Kind of a way of testing to see what would happen if they threw this kind of bait into the water with no past data to work from.

With this much experimentation taking place on the part of so many people, fear of missing out becomes a key driver and drives everything rapidly to the point of saturation. What happens after that saturation point is what we should all be concerned about, but this is everyone's first time doing this. So nobody knows what's will take place.

Mow has also stated that NFTs have a lot of untapped potential yet to be explored, especially when it comes to art and gaming. If NFTs were fully applied to aspects of gaming, the successful implementer would rake in hundreds of billions each year.

But he closes his statement by saying that the long-term worth of an NFT is probably nonexistent. A lot of NFTs are tied to the reputation of the people who made them. Take, for example, *NBA Top Shot*. Its novelty made people go nuts over the moments they could buy, like animated sports cards. But when you buy one of those moments as an NFT, you don't gain any special privileges. You don't own the copyright, and you don't get any commercial distribution rights. All you've really gained is a copy of the video clip. As of this time, there's no reason to believe that a copy of a video clip will be worth more down the road than it is at this moment. The manufacturer's scarcity that has driven up the value of these entities may not be enough to sustain that value in the long term.

Nithin Palavalli Is the chief executive officer at Rubik's. He feels that NFTs have nearly unlimited potential in applications far outside what they're being used in today. Industries such as luxury, textiles, pharmaceutical, shipping, supply chain management are all areas of business that depend on accurate and immutable information that could make use of NFT technology, especially concerning the blockchain.

<u>Conclusion</u>

Thank you for joining me on this journey through the lively and very much developing world of NFTs. Everything you've just read is the current understanding of how to realistically cash in on the phenomenon.

What do you think at this point? There's no questioning the fact that there is some quick cash to be made. But the likelihood of making money seems to come to those willing to spend some time putting in work. And yet, time may not be on the NFT investor's side, as technology, regulations, and the whims of buyers and collectors change.

Because, after all, it's those whims that are driving the value of the NFT market right now. That's such a critical point that it's worth repeating.

The ultimate determining factor of the value of NFTs right now is what people are willing to pay for them.

It sounds arbitrary, but it's the truth. People do not stay the same. Their likes and their preferences are not going to stay the same. So the NFT market is going to change eventually. It's not a matter of *if*, it's a matter of *when*.

So you have to decide if you're going to go out on a limb to try to make a million bucks quickly, or if you're going to gamble on the possibility that the buzz that's active now will be there later, and put in some steady, solid work. And guess what? At the end of the day, this is nothing new in the realm of investment. NFTs today are being leveraged to the maximum by the "day traders," but maybe their future will be the most beneficial to the Warren Buffets of the world. Who knows. You just have to decide which one you're going to be for now.

<u>Works Cited</u>

"Are NFTs a Good Long Term Investment? On Ownership & Long-Term Viability: Finance Magnates." *Finance Magnates | Financial and Business News*, Finance Magnates, 4 May 2021, www.financemagnates.com/cryptocurrency/news/are-nfts-a-good-long-term-investment-on-ownership-long-term-viability/.

Binance Academy. "How to Make Your Own NFTs." *Binance Academy*, Binance Academy, 6 Aug. 2021, www.academy.binance.com/en/articles/how-to-make-your-own-nfts.

Brad Bulent Yasar, FollowBlockchain & Cryptocurrency Advisor, and Follow. "A Brief History of NFTs and a Look into the Future." *LinkedIn*, www.linkedin.com/pulse/brief-history-nfts-look-future-brad-bulent-yasar/.

Clark, Mitchell. "NFTs Explained." *The Verge*, The Verge, 3 Mar. 2021, www.theverge.com/22310188/nft-explainer-what-is-blockchain-crypto-art-faq.

Coggan, Georgia. "Confused about NFTs? Here's All You Need to Know." *Creative Bloq*, Creative Bloq, 25 June 2021, www.creativebloq.com/features/what-are-nfts.

Conti, Robyn. "What You Need to Know about Non-Fungible Tokens (NFTs)." *Forbes*, Forbes Magazine, 23 June 2021, www.forbes.com/advisor/investing/nft-non-fungible-token.

Contributor. "Setting the Record Straight on NFTs, the Most Misunderstood Financial Advancement in History." *VentureBeat*, VentureBeat, 19 May 2021, www.venturebeat.com/2021/05/20/setting-the-record-straight-on-nfts-the-most-misunderstood-financial-advancement-in-history.

Haselton, Todd. "How to Make, Buy and Sell NFTs." *CNBC*, CNBC, 24 Mar. 2021, www.cnbc.com/2021/03/23/how-to-create-buy-sell-nfts.html.

Made in United States
North Haven, CT
08 December 2021

12128708R10072